Here and There
(or maybe elsewhere)

Lilith Bastet

BookLeaf
Publishing

India | USA | UK

Presentation by *BookLeaf Publishing*

Web: www.bookleafpub.com

E-mail: info@bookleafpub.com

ISBN: 978-93-5744-986-1

First edition 2022

DEDICATION

To people I miss

To People I miss
(2016)

Yes, I sometimes forget
about you,
and us,
and my life,
as busy as my mind,
does not give much space
to you
and us
to nostalgia.

But sometimes, sometimes,
memories as bright
as when we lived them
come and remind me
of you
and us
so painfully
it makes me happy
like the face of a loved one
in a crowd of strangers.

Time fades away
like you

and us
but my thoughts are still
floating
around you
and us
like vapors of the past.

Behind Every Hello
a Goodbye Hides
(2021)

Of all the lessons that life has taught me,
There is one I wish that I did not know:
It is that places and people,
They always come and go.

Let me tell You,
You who are listening:
The truth is that any new beginning
Is also the beginning of the end
So that behind every hello a goodbye hides,
And in every neighbor, companion, or friend
Awaits a final hug that already cries.

Make no mistakes, for even your lovers
In short, everyone you care about
Will, without a doubt,
One day turn back into strangers.
You'd better accept it, and beware:
For it will not get easier, nor become fair.

Last night I dreamt I was already dead
(2021)

It was nice and quiet.
You were not there,
Though.
I don't know where you were.
Maybe you took my place, right here
Laying in bed, wishing you'd disappear.
Just for some time,
Just for one long night...
But I know two wrongs could never make a
right.

So I tell myself it is not so bad,
After all.
That I am not unlucky,
(No more than any other, anyway)
Just ungrateful.
That the starving children
And the wounded soldiers
They are laughing at me!
There is enough sorrow for everybody
So why do I like to pretend it is all mine?

So I tried to dream of things that are happy
Of fresh air, of blue skies, and sunshine
Of us together, smiling, and healthy
But I could not fall asleep.

Untitled 1
(2021)

Good memories aren't like good wine:
They don't age well.

The ones that remain turn sour
From being replayed over and over in your head
A little less vividly each time.
Nostalgia does that to good things.

The ones that fade away still feel bitter
Like these medicines that leave you with a rusty
aftertaste
Even long after you've swallowed them.
Forgetfulness is no remedy.

Remember, or don't
What was once sweet will turn rancid either
way.

Time

(2020)

"Wait!"
I said,
"Wait!"
But Time doesn't wait.

"Come back!" I cried
But It kept on going Its way:
Forward.

Until It was far, far away...
Gone, and me with It.

Pantoum
(2019)

It is cold, in your absence
As if the Sun had forgotten to rise
And deafening is you silence
When all I can hear are my cries

As if the Sun had forgotten to rise,
My nights feel longer
When all I can hear are my cries
In the morning sky of winter.

My nights feel longer
Ever since you have been gone.
In the morning sky of winter,
Life without you must go on.

Ever since you have been gone,
Deafening is your silence.
Life, without you, must go on
It is cold, in your absence.

Shh!!
(2021)

Tonight
I don't want to talk
I don't want to say what's wrong
And I couldn't talk about anything else anyway

Leave me alone
So that I can listen to my silence
Like others do to music
I couldn't listen to anything else anyway

I don't want to talk!!
I said
Isn't that enough??
It is too much for me already
Seven words too many
Shh! Shh!
I don't want to say,
I said,
I
don't
want
to
say!!

But I think about it all the time
I think about it all the time
I think about it all the time I think about it all the
time I think about it all the time I THINK
ABOUT IT ALL THE TIME I THINK ABOUT
IT ALL THE TIMEITHINKABOUTITALL
THETIMEITHINKITHINKABOUTITALLTHE
TIMEITHINKABOUTITALLTHEITHINK

When will I be home?
(2021)

For now I am here,
But only for now.
Soon, I will be elsewhere -
There? Maybe,
Or some other place.

When will I be home?

Flowers of Silence
(2015/2020)

I waited for you all night
But only the morning came.
As the sun rose, rose the light
Burning my eyes like a flame.

I wanted to tell you-,
But no.
I have no more words to say.
As that which remains unsaid
Can last longer than the finest prose
And there lies in the silences ahead
Much more than words could ever disclose.

Because every feeling, every sentiment
Is mostly implied,
I will not let my chagrin, nor my resentment
Make the slightest sound.

So I wait
Wait until it is not too late
Anymore
As if time cared about us…

Burnt Love
(2015)

If everything must taste like ashes
I'd rather it be ashes of you
Ashes of our love
Still burning
Somewhere we are not
Anymore

Only the smoke I see
Rising up in the night
Look how it dances
Look how it twirls
Right before it dissipates

We still had air and wood and dedication
For a while the fire could have kept burning
Only time we missed
Now it's you I miss.

Untitled 2
(2020)

When I think of you I cry
When I don't, I cry
But I don't know why.

I may have forgotten everything -
Your face
Your words
Your voice
Everything
But the pain of losing you.

That, I remember
Over and over.

Untitled 3
(2021)

There are people who
Grow like trees:
Firmly rooted,
Feet on the ground,
With their head held high,
Always looking up to the sky.
I envy them.

I, grow more like a vine.
I have no stable trunk to support me
But rather many flexible stems
That find their way through the cracks
In every direction there is to explore.
Sometimes,
I cannot tell up from down anymore.

Hopeless
(2020)

I hate Hope.
It keeps me going
In times when
I don't want to keep going
Anymore.

It makes me look forward
When I am stuck in the now
And paralyzed.

Hope makes me miss
Things I have never even had
And regret things that
Have not even happened
Yet.

Hope
 Is full of longing
And empty promises.
My failures, my despair, my own lack of
prospects
That, I could face.
Oh! How I wish I was hopeless.

I think, maybe
(2014)

I think, maybe
In a world next to mine
The sound of my tears is silent
And sweetness has replaced the bitter taste of
my memories.

The past is far, and the present as well
But the future is bright and full of stories to tell.

I think there is something
else,
somewhere
else,
But they say one cannot miss
What one has never known.

So maybe I am wrong,
Maybe there is nothing right
And if this is all there is,
Then maybe it is not so bad.

Winter Poem
(2017/2021)

Today,
Let my thoughts be darker
Than the morning sky of winter.

Let my words fall like hail,
Hurt like hell,
Let them fail once again.
They fail me,
And you,
And inside, just like outside,
The cold found us.

The air is icy
My mind, foggy
And, suddenly
I catch myself dreaming of summer.
Will you, as the sun will,
One day return, and stay still?

Untitled 4

(2021)

For a while
I used to walk the wide boulevards of Paris
To which I was so used to
I forgot to look up to the white buildings
With their grey metal roofs
That make the rain so loud to those who listen .
I liked the pigeons there
It always appeared to me that
They were never dirty,
But rather sullied.
Perhaps in the forest we would call them doves.

Then
I erred in the narrow paved streets of
Amsterdam
With its many many canals
That look like streets of their own
And their many more bridges
Made of burgundy bricks.
I can still feel the wind blow in my hair
And hear the church bells ring
(or is it the bikes?)
But I forgot the sound of my friends' voices.

Now
I wander around London's busy roads and empty
mews
Where rainy days don't feel grey but rather
brown
Like old leather and smoky gravy.
At night the foxes scream
I hear them when I am not asleep.

Still, there are moments when
I think back to the wide white boulevards
And burgundy bricks and bridges
And I ask myself, where did they all go?

The Seine, the Amstel, the Thames
They just keep flowing.
They wouldn't stop for anything - or anybody,
really
Let alone a lonely me.

Is it Time I see?
(2021)

Look! Is it Time I see, running around in panic?
Why the hurry?
He smiled and turned to me:
"It's funny", He said. "Everyone keeps asking
me that."
"But, has it occured to you, that, perhaps,
Someone is waiting for me?
Her name is Patience."
I wanted to tell him that She would come soon,
If only He would stop right here,
But already, He had run away.

For now
(2021)

For now I am here.
It isn't much,
But it is all there is.

Soon,
They will all be back:
The white walls, empty spaces,
Busy mind and heavy heart.
Boxes all packed and stacked,
Waiting for someplace new -
Then why does it always feel more like an end
Than a fresh beginning?

But, for now I am here.
It isn't much,
But it is all there is.

www.ingramcontent.com/pod-product-compliance
Lightning Source LLC
LaVergne TN
LVHW050300200726
843509LV00015B/3088